The Apache

by Petra Press

Content Adviser: Professor Sherry L. Field,
Department of Social Science Education, College of Education,
The University of Georgia

Reading Adviser: Dr. Linda D. Labbo,
Department of Reading Education, College of Education,
The University of Georgia

COMPASS POINT BOOKS

Minneapolis, Minnesota

FIRST REPORTS

Compass Point Books
3722 West 50th Street, #115
Minneapolis, MN 55410

Visit Compass Point Books on the Internet at *www.compasspointbooks.com* or e-mail your request to *custserv@compasspointbooks.com*

Front cover: Apache basket, San Carlos Apache Cultural Museum

Photographs ©: Marilyn "Angel" Wynn, cover, 4, 5, 9, 10, 11, 15, 16, 17, 19, 25, 31, 35, 38, 39, 40, 41, 42, 43; XNR Productions, 7; Arthur Morris/Visuals Unlimited, 8; North Wind Picture Archives, 12, 20, 26; Denver Public Library, Western History Collection, 13, 18, 28, 32, 33, 34, 36, 37; Hulton Getty/Archive Photos, 14, 24, 29; Stock Montage, 21, 27; Archive Photos: 22, 23, 30.

Editors: E. Russell Primm, Emily J. Dolbear, and Alice K. Flanagan
Photo Researcher: Svetlana Zhurkina
Photo Selector: Catherine Neitge
Designer: Bradfordesign, Inc.

Library of Congress Cataloging-in-Publication Data
Press, Petra.
    The Apache / by Petra Press.
        p. cm. — (First reports)
    Includes bibliographical references and index.
    ISBN 0-7565-0077-X (hardcover : lib. bdg.)
    1. Apache Indians—History—Juvenile literature. 2. Apache Indians—Social life and customs—Juvenile literature. [1. Apache Indians. 2. Indians of North America—New Mexico.] I. Title. II. Series.
E99.A6 .P74 2001
979'.004972—dc21   00-011064

Table of Contents

▲ *An Apache dancer in Gallup, New Mexico*

4

Who Are the Apache?

The Apache (pronounced uh-PA-chee) are Native Americans. They live mostly in the mountains and deserts of the southwestern United States and north-western Mexico.

▲ *Cacti dot the rough land in the southwestern United States.*

There are six Apache tribes. They are the Mescalero, Jicarilla, Chiricahua, Lipan, Kiowa, and Western Apache.

Each Apache tribe has its own way of life. Each tribe speaks a form of the same language. All the Apache tribes are proud of their past.

The Apache once lived far north. They lived in what is now Alaska and northwestern Canada.

Between A.D. 850 and 1000, the Apache moved south. They moved to the southwestern United States, which is also called the Southwest. They came looking for food and warmer weather.

▲ A map of past and present Apache lands

Traveling Hunters

A long time ago, the Apache were **nomads**. Nomads are people who travel from place to place in search of food.

The Apache hunted antelope, buffalo, deer, wild turkeys, and lizards. They also gathered wild plants. They ate mesquite beans, cactus fruit, and acorns.

▲ *The Apache hunted wild turkey.*

▲ *The Apache gathered cactus fruit.*

Some Apache were farmers as well as hunters. But they still moved from place to place. They planted corn, pumpkins, beans, onions, and potatoes. Then they came back to gather the crops.

The Apache made good use of the animals they hunted. The men made tools, weapons, and toys out of animal bones. The women dried the meat for other meals. And they made clothing from the animal skins.

▲ Apache shoes, or moccasins

Women also made baskets. They were called burden baskets because they made women's burdens, or duties, lighter. The women kept dried food, clothing, and firewood in these baskets. They also wove baskets tightly enough to carry water.

▲ *A woman in traditional Apache clothing carries a burden basket.*

Many Apache lived in **wickiups**. These were dome-shaped huts. They were made of wooden poles covered with branches and grasses or animal skins.

The Mescalero and Kiowa Apache lived in tepees. These were cone-shaped tents made of buffalo skin or deerskin and wooden poles.

▲ *Some Apache lived in dome-shaped huts called wickiups.*

▲ *A Mescalero Apache camp in New Mexico in the 1880s*

Tepees and wickiups were perfect houses for nomads. They could put them up and take them down easily. They could carry tepees and wickiups from place to place.

The Importance of Family

▲ An Apache baby in 1900

The Apache lived in a rough land. They needed one another. So Apache families traveled together. They also lived near each other. Parents, children, grandparents, uncles, and aunts built their wickiups close together.

Apache families chose a head man to lead their group. The group was known by this man's name. Sometimes families got together to help one another. They were called a **band**.

Bands had **councils** with leaders from each family group. The council made big decisions. It decided when to go to war.

Apache bands never had just one leader. The Apache never had just one chief. They did not act as a single group. One Apache band might make peace with an enemy. That did not mean that all bands agreed to peace.

▲ *Wickiups were built close together.*

Apache Religion

Religion was an important part of Apache life. The Apache believed in a creator. They also believed that spirits lived in everything. They believed that spirits lived in animals, plants, rocks, rivers, and even the sky. Some spirits were good, and some were evil.

▲ Apache ceremonial grounds

▲ *The Apache use sticks during ceremonies.*

People who could talk to the spirits were called **shamans**. Shamans danced and sang songs for the spirits. They asked the spirits to help hunters and **warriors**. They often asked the spirits to help heal the sick.

Shamans held special **ceremonies**. They welcomed new children into the family. They also honored children when they became adults.

When a boy was about thirteen years old, he went on his first attack to capture horses. If he did well, he was taught warrior secrets. When a girl was about thirteen, a ceremony was held for her. It was called Changing Woman.

▲ *A Chiricahua Apache shaman and his family inside their wickiup in about 1885*

Apache Warriors

When the Apache came to the Southwest, other Native Americans were living there. The Pueblo had been living in the Southwest for many years.

At first, the Apache and the Pueblo lived in peace. They traded with each other. The Apache traded buffalo hides, meat, and bones. The Pueblo traded pottery, cotton, blankets, and corn.

▲ *The rugged mountains of Arizona in the Southwest*

Finding food in the mountains and deserts was hard. Sometimes, there was very little to eat. Then Apache men attacked Pueblo villages and stole food. Later, they stole horses.

In time, the Apache became known as warriors. They fought to protect their families. They also attacked people who had killed tribe members.

▲ *An Apache warrior gets rattlesnake poison for his arrows.*

The Spaniards

In 1540, a Spaniard named Francisco de Coronado came to the Southwest. He and his soldiers explored the area. They rode horses and carried guns.

The Apache watched how the strangers rode the horses. Before long, the Apache learned to ride

▲ *Spaniard Francisco de Coronado and his men explored the Southwest in 1540.*

horses too. Then they began stealing horses and guns from the Spanish villages.

With horses and guns, the Apache became better hunters. They also became more dangerous warriors.

Some Apache lived near the Spaniards. They became ill from European diseases. They were treated badly by the Spaniards. Many Apache died.

▲ *Apache warriors*

A New Enemy

The Apache had many enemies. Their enemies were the Spaniards, the Mexicans, and many other Native American tribes. The Apache fought off these enemies. Then they met an enemy that they could not beat.

This new enemy was the United States of America. In 1848, the United States won a war against Mexico.

▲ *The United States defeated Mexico in 1848.*

Much of today's Arizona and New Mexico became part of the United States. The Apache were now under U.S. control.

In 1849, gold was discovered in California. Hundreds of Americans traveled west to get rich. On the way, they passed through Apache land.

▲ *Gold was discovered at Sutter's Mill in California in 1849.*

▲ *Teddy bear cactus on the Apache Trail in Arizona*

At first, the Apache were friendly. They let the Americans pass. Sometimes they even helped them find water. But then the Americans began to take over Apache land. The Apache fought back.

The Apache Wars

▲ *An Apache on horseback takes aim.*

One of the Apache leaders was named Cochise. In 1861, U.S. soldiers put him in prison. The U.S. government said that Cochise had taken a settler's child. They also said that Cochise had attacked their soldiers.

These things were not true. Cochise escaped from prison. The U.S. government hanged his brother and two nephews. Cochise and the Apache fought with the United States. The fighting was called the Apache Wars.

The Apache were excellent warriors, but they did not win the wars. They knew every inch of their homeland. They had good leaders and fast horses, but the United States had more soldiers and better weapons.

▲ *U.S. soldiers had better weapons than the Apache.*

▲ *Nachez, the son of Cochise, in 1884*

In 1876, the United States ordered the Apache onto **reservations**. Reservations were large areas of land set aside for Native Americans to live on. Many Apache moved to the White Mountain and San Carlos Reservations in Arizona.

Cochise agreed to stop fighting. He would move his band to a reservation in Arizona. Many Apache bands refused to give up their way of life. They fought U.S. troops for another thirteen years.

Geronimo

▲ *Geronimo, far right, and his men*

One strong Apache leader did not want to give up. The Mexicans called him Geronimo. His Apache name was Goyathlay. That means "one who yawns."

Geronimo had not always been a warrior. Once he was a hunter and trader. But in 1850, Mexican soldiers

▲ *Hattie Tom, a member of Geronimo's band, was a baby when the group gave up.*

killed Geronimo's mother, wife, and children. They also killed twenty-two people in his band. Then they sold another seventy as slaves. That day, Geronimo became a warrior for his people.

Geronimo was a brave leader. Many Apache fought with him. They attacked U.S. forts. They tried to drive out white settlers.

The U.S. Army sent 5,000 soldiers after Geronimo. On September 4, 1886, Geronimo's group gave up. Only sixteen warriors, twelve women, and six children were left.

▲ *Geronimo*

Geronimo and his followers were sent to Florida as prisoners. Later, they were moved to Oklahoma. Geronimo never saw his homeland again.

Reservation Life

▲ *An Apache family sits in front of its wickiup in Arizona in about 1885.*

By 1890, most Apache lived on reservations. There were five reservations. The Fort Apache (now called the White Mountain) and San Carlos Reservations were in Arizona. The Jicarilla and Mescalero Reservations were in New Mexico. The Fort Sill Reservation was in Oklahoma.

Reservation life was hard. The people did not have enough food, clothing, or tools. They could not hunt as they once did. Many people died of disease and bad food. Some Apache tried to farm, but the crops didn't grow well.

Soon, white settlers wanted the Apache land. They wanted to feed their animals on the land. They

▲ *Apache men and boys in their camp along the San Carlos River in Arizona in the 1880s*

▲ A Kiowa Apache tepee camp near Fort Sill, Oklahoma, in the late 1800s

wanted to mine the land. So the U.S. government sold them some of the Apache land.

Over time, more and more white settlers came. They wanted even more land. In 1887, the U.S. government passed a law. This law gave each Native American family 160 acres (65 hectares) to farm. The U.S. government sold the rest of the land to white settlers.

▲ *Apache Lake in the Tonto National Forest in Arizona*

A New Way of Life

During the 1890s, the U.S. government took Apache children away from their families. The children were sent to **boarding schools**. Some schools were hundreds of miles away.

▲ Chiricahua Apache boys and girls outside the Carlisle Indian School in Pennsylvania after coming from Fort Marion, Florida, in 1886

At these special schools, the children dressed like American children. They were not allowed to speak their language. They had to speak English. They could not follow their Indian traditions. Before long, the Apache children lost pride in their Indian way of life.

▲ *The same boys and girls four months later*

▲ Apache basket makers in San Carlos, Arizona, in 1907

In 1924, the U.S. government made all Native Americans citizens of the United States of America. After that, reservation life started to get better. The government spent more money on health care for Native Americans. It started to build them better schools.

Ten years later, the U.S. government passed another law. This law helped Native Americans set up their own governments to run the reservations. It also helped them start businesses.

▲ *An Apache woman plays the fiddle.*

The Apache Today

▲ *A young girl rides a horse on the White Mountain Reservation.*

Today, life is much better for the Apache. But there is still a lot to be done.

The Apache are proud of their traditions. But they also believe that modern ways will make their lives better. They want good schools for their children. They want good jobs for themselves.

Jobs are hard to find on the reservations, however. Some people work in the gas stations, restaurants, and laundries on the reservations. Others work as ranchers, farmers, and lumber-mill workers.

The Mescalero and the White Mountain Apache run ski resorts. Several Apache **casinos** are successful.

▲ *Apache run the Sunrise Ski Resort in eastern Arizona.*

Many Apache have earned college degrees. They work as doctors, lawyers, and teachers on the reservations.

But most of the Apache are still very poor. They need better housing. They need more opportunities for their children. Their future depends on it.

▲ An Apache casino near Payson, Arizona

▲ *A Jicarilla Apache silversmith shows his beautiful jewelry.*

Glossary

band—a group of people who live and travel together

boarding schools—schools where students live

casinos—places where people bet money on games of chance

ceremonies—formal actions to mark an important time

councils—groups of people chosen to make important decisions

nomads—people who move in groups in search of food

reservations—large areas of land set aside for Native Americans; in Canada, reservations are called reserves

shamans—people who try to contact the spirit world and are skilled in curing illnesses

warriors—people trained to fight in battles

wickiups—dome-shaped huts made of poles covered with grasses and reeds or animal skins

Did You Know?

- The name *Apache* may have come from a Zuni word for "enemy."

- In traditional Apache families, mothers-in-law are forbidden to speak to their sons-in-law.

- Before the Apache had horses, they used dogs to carry their belongings.

- Arizona has a county named after Cochise.

At a Glance

Tribal name: Apache

Divisions: Mescalero, Jicarilla, Chiricahua, Lipan, Kiowa, Western Apache

Past locations: Alaska, Arizona, New Mexico, Colorado, Oklahoma, Texas, Mexico, northwestern Canada

Present locations: Arizona, New Mexico, Oklahoma, Mexico

Traditional houses: Dome-shaped huts called wickiups and cone-shaped tents called tepees

Traditional clothing materials: Deerskin; later, cotton and wool trade goods

Traditional transportation: Feet; later, horses

Traditional food: Deer, buffalo, antelope, cactus, acorns

Important Dates

A.D. 850–1000	Apache groups move to the southwestern United States from northwestern Canada and Alaska.
1540	A Spaniard named Francisco de Coronado explores the Southwest.
1848	Mexico loses to the United States in the Mexican War. It gives up land that includes Apache country.
1861	U.S. soldiers put Apache leader Cochise in prison.
1876	The United States orders the Apache onto reservations.
1861–1886	Apache Wars take place.
1886	Apache warrior Geronimo surrenders to the U.S. Army.
1890s	The U.S. government takes Apache children away from their families.
1940s	The Apache sue the U.S. government seeking payment for their stolen land.
1970	The Jicarilla are given $10 million by the Indian Claims Commission.

Want to Know More?

At the Library

Claro, Nicole. *The Apache Indians*. New York: Chelsea House, 1992.

McCall, Barbara. *The Apache*. Vero Beach, Fla.: Rourke Publishing Group, 1990.

Sneve, Virginia Driving Hawk. *The Apaches*. New York: Holiday House, 1997.

On the Web

Geronimo: His Own Story
http://odur.let.rug.nl/~usa/B/geronimo/geronixx.htm
For Geronimo's story in his own words

White Mountain Apache of Arizona
http://www.cybertrails.com/~azboater/index.html
For pictures, student artwork, and recipes from a fifth-grade class on the Fort Apache Reservation

Through the Mail

San Carlos Apache Tribe
P.O. Box 0
San Carlos, AZ 85550
To get more information about the tribe

On the Road

San Carlos Apache Cultural Center
P.O. Box 760
Peridot, AZ 85542
520/475-2894
Located near milepost 272 on Highway 70
To experience past and present Apache life, hear music and legends, and see crafts and photographs

Index

About the Author

Petra Press is a freelance writer of young adult
nonfiction, specializing in the diverse culture of the
Americas. Her more than twenty books include histories
of U.S. immigration, education, and settlement of the
West, as well as portraits of numerous indigenous
cultures. She lives with her husband, David, in
Milwaukee, Wisconsin.